Original title:
Tropical Bliss

Copyright © 2025 Creative Arts Management OÜ
All rights reserved.

Author: Benjamin Caldwell
ISBN HARDBACK: 978-1-80581-567-9
ISBN PAPERBACK: 978-1-80581-094-0
ISBN EBOOK: 978-1-80581-567-9

Radiant Blooms and Ocean Whispers

A parrot squawks, a crab does dance,
The flowers bloom, they take a chance.
Sunburned tourists laugh and trip,
While sipping drinks with funny quips.

The waves come in, they splash about,
With seagulls diving, never a doubt.
Sand stuck in toes, a price to pay,
For memories made on a sunny day.

Journey Through the Emerald Jungle

In the jungle, vines twist and twine,
A monkey swings, says 'Is this mine?'
The humidity clings like a cheeky friend,
While tourists' hats are on the mend.

Lizards chase bugs, they're quite the sight,
Chasing shadows in the fading light.
With a slip and a slide, oh what a mess,
As we trek through the green, no time to stress.

Beneath the Shade of Palatial Trees

Under the trees where the cool breeze flows,
A squirrel steals snacks, he likes to pose.
Our picnic spread, a feast gone wild,
With ants joining in, they're so beguiled.

Laughter erupts as a drink can spills,
The sun peeks through, bringing more thrills.
Everyone's sweating, yet still we grin,
In this shady spot, the fun won't thin.

The Melody of Hummingbirds and Heat

The hummingbirds dart, a blur of hue,
While I just stand, feeling quite askew.
With sweat on my brow and a laugh so hearty,
Saying 'No regrets!' at this wild party.

A coconut falls, it rolls with flair,
A nearby sunbather shows he doesn't care.
As we dance to the rhythm, in flip-flops we sway,
Chasing the sun through the beat of the day.

Lush Greens and Azure Dreams

In the jungle where the monkeys swing,
A parrot jokes about a banana fling.
Plants in riot, green from top to toe,
Tickling toes where the funny flowers grow.

Frogs in tuxedos leap with flair,
While iguanas lounge without a care.
Every leaf whispers, 'Are we in a play?'
Nature's comedy, brightening the day.

A Dance of Sunbeams

Sunshine's waltz makes the shadows dance,
With flip-flops flapping, we take a chance.
Coconuts are drumming, rhythms so fine,
While crabs in shades wear a funny line.

The surfboards slide, the laughter's loud,
Seagulls squawk jokes to the colorful crowd.
As the waves tickle toes on the shore,
Every splash is a giggle, who could ask for more?

Ocean Spray and Heartfelt Laughter

The ocean sprays with a salty kiss,
While fish in tuxedos plot their bliss.
Jellyfish in hats, so grand and bright,
Dancing under the moon, oh, what a sight!

A clam tells a joke, the others just gawk,
As dolphins gather for a silly talk.
Together we splash, like kids in a game,
In this watery world, we're all the same.

Whispers of the Gentle Breeze

The breeze carries secrets, oh-so-sweet,
Whispers of laughter, a rhythm on repeat.
Palm trees sway like they're grooving along,
While the sand sings a silly, cheerful song.

Flowers giggle as the butterflies flirt,
While children build castles from sun-kissed dirt.
Each moment sprawls out, a canvas so bright,
In this paradise, everything feels just right.

A Choir of Morning Birds

Early morn, the singers stir,
Feathers ruffle, melodies blur.
A crow croaks like a rusty hinge,
A tune that makes the flowers cringe.

Sparrows chat in squeaky tones,
While seagulls squawk on sandy stones.
Their harmonies seem quite absurd,
A symphony of chaos heard.

The Colorful Tides of Paradise

Waves that crash wear goofy grins,
Beneath, a world where mischief spins.
Red crabs dance in wobbly lines,
While starfish practice funky signs.

Surfboards fly like birds in flight,
But wipeouts cause a silly sight.
The ocean laughs, its frothy glee,
In hues of yellow, blue, and pea.

Raindrops and Sunshine Dance.

Raindrops twirl in the sun's embrace,
Dancing wildly, what a race!
Puddles splatter, kids abound,
Kicking water all around.

Sunshine giggles from above,
While rain gives earth a bubbly love.
Together they create a show,
A wet and wild, bright, shining glow.

Island Serenades

Coconuts drop with a thunk and roll,
While monkeys steal the limelight goal.
Tropical tunes played by a goat,
Making melodies from a boat.

A parrot squawks, 'You're out of tune!'
As palm trees sway to the afternoon.
Laughter echoes through the trees,
Island life is a breeze, with ease.

Driftwood Memories

On the beach, a stick did dance,
Carried by waves, it took a chance.
It rolled around with such delight,
Chasing crabs 'til the fall of night.

Once it tried to ride a wave,
Screaming, 'Help!' it thought it brave.
But back to shore, it tumbled down,
Now it's the king with a crown of brown.

The Comfort of Warm Sun

Sunning on the golden sand,
I spotted fries, oh isn't that grand?
A seagull swooped, I took a dive,
Now fries fly high and I just survive.

The sun's embrace, a toaster's dream,
Melting my plans with its warm beam.
Yet the shade calls, with cooler glee,
Just as the ice cream calls to me.

Serene Horizons and Gentle Currents

Horizons whisper nautical tales,
Where fish wear hats and swim in pails.
The gentle currents hum a song,
Of mermaids who say, 'You can't go wrong.'

Floating by with a coconut drink,
I ponder life, and start to think,
If fish could dance like we all do,
Would they wear shoes? I'd love a view!

Blissful Retreats by the Water

In my hammock, I sway with ease,
Waves serenade, a gentle tease.
But a squirrel thinks it's time to play,
And steals my snack, then scurries away.

Sunsets spill like ice cream drops,
While laughter tumbles from friendly shops.
With each splash, my troubles fade,
In this paradise, fun's homemade.

Echoes of the Island Heart

In a hammock laid, I doze and dream,
While a rooster crows, it's quite the scheme.
A coconut falls with a thud and a splash,
Turning peaceful snooze into a frantic dash.

Crabs dance on the shore, they think they can prance,
While I sip my drink, they steal my chance.
A parrot laughs loud, in the hues of the sun,
Saying 'loosen up, mate, it's time to have fun!'

Morning Mist Over the Lagoon

Misty rivers swirl, like a ghost at dawn,
A sunburnt tourist stumbles and fawn.
Frogs croak a tune, but don't get it right,
The fish give a chuckle, diving out of sight.

A kayak floats by, but it's stuck on a log,
While a dolphin jumps high, and it starts to hog.
With coffee in hand, the day starts to glow,
As I spill it all over, oh no, here we go!

Swaying Palms in the Moonlight

The palms dance a jig, swaying left and right,
While I trip on my flip-flops, what a silly sight!
A crab in my path, he holds up a sign,
'Please give me some space, I'm too cool, divine!'

Moonlight kisses the beach, I try to impress,
But I slip in the sand and fall in a mess.
Laughter erupts from the waves as they roll,
'Don't worry, friend, it's good for your soul!'

Ocean's Embrace at Twilight

As the sun takes a bow, and the sky glows bright,
I'm ready to dance, feeling tipsy with delight.
The waves share a joke, they bubble and churn,
But I'm here to wiggle, it's my turn to learn.

A fish in a tux, waves from below,
He's mocking my moves, it's putting on a show.
So I do the cha-cha, under starlit beams,
As the ocean chuckles, dancing all my dreams.

The Essence of Paradise in Every Breath

Sipping coconut water, oh what a delight,
Sunburn on my nose, but my heart feels light.
Hammock swings low, with a giggle or two,
Crabs join the dance, as they waddle on through.

Flip-flops are flapping, they never quite match,
Seagulls steal fries, it's a comical catch.
With each wave that rolls, I'm losing my score,
Did I drop my pink drink? Oh, not on the floor!

Palm trees are dancing, they sway here and there,
While I try to juggle my sunscreen and hair.
Flip-flops to the left, my towel to the right,
These memories I make, will be pure comic sight.

As sunset approaches, my dance gets the cheer,
I trip on my towel, but I've nothing to fear.
In this laughter-infused, sun-kissed charade,
The essence of joy, in this paradise made.

Echoes of Tropical Hearts

In hammocks swinging, we lay with glee,
A parrot squawks jokes, talking to a bee.
Coconuts chuckle, rolling on the sand,
While sunburned tourists dance like a band.

The waves join in, with a splash and a spray,
Telling tales of crabs who jive all day.
A coconut drink spills all over my leg,
And the punchline's lost, like an old rusty peg.

Seagulls and Sunsets

Seagulls swoop down, with sass and a spin,
Stealing my fries, oh where do I begin?
As sunsets paint skies in a wild, loud hue,
We laugh at the gulls, it's just what they do.

With chips on our laps, we share silly grins,
As seagulls plot ways to steal all our wins.
The sun dips down, it's a comic display,
We cheer for the dusk with a 'Life's quite okay!'

The Story of a Forgotten Cove

There's a cove down south, lost in a tale,
Where flip-flops whisper, and fish tell the scale.
A crab pulls a prank, pinching toes with delight,
While sandcastles grumble, 'We're falling tonight!'

The sun takes a dip, and so do the clams,
As I chase a fish, it just wiggles and slams.
Forgotten for ages, yet full of such fun,
That cove guffaws, under the warm setting sun.

A Symphony in Nature's Arms

A symphony plays with each palm tree sway,
Where frogs croak a beat, come join in the play.
Monkeys throw coconuts, actors on stage,
While dancing iguanas, let loose with a rage.

The breeze sings a tune, a whistle so bright,
As the sun winks at us, igniting the night.
With laughter as music, we skip without care,
Nature's loud laughter resounds through the air.

Heartbeats of the Ocean

The waves hum a tune, so bright,
A seagull croons, what a sight.
Fish dance below, in a silly show,
Wiggling their tails, oh what a delight.

Who knew the sea had such flair?
With crabs in tuxedos, they declare,
"Join our parade, it's quite the charade,
Life's just a splash, with laughter to share."

Beach balls bounce like wayward dreams,
Chasing the sun, slipping through beams.
A clam in a grin, says, "Let's begin!"
As joy spills out in salty streams.

So raise your drink, let's toast and cheer,
To flip-flops and sunscreen, never fear!
For the ocean's giggle, and sand's warm tickle,
Bring giggles and grins, all through the year.

A Tapestry of Colorful Blooms

Petals dance like they're in a play,
Roses leaning in for a bouquet.
Lilies exchange winks, quite the prank,
Sunflowers stretch, saying, "Hip-hip-hooray!"

Bees buzz by, in a dizzy trance,
Pollinating like they're on a chance.
Daisies shout, 'Hey, look at me!'
In this garden, they all do their dance.

A gnome drops his hat, what a sight!
As blooms start to giggle, pure delight.
Tulips smirk, 'We're dressed to impress,'
In a patchwork sky, they shine so bright.

Every leaf whispers secrets to bees,
As butterflies tease with a flutter and tease.
Together they sing, oh what a fling,
Amidst all the color, they're hard to appease.

Enchantment in Every Tide

The ocean's wave has a quirky side,
Pulling your toes like a fun ride.
Barnacles snicker as they cling on tight,
To this wild ballet that the sea had supplied.

Surfers tumble, oh what a sight,
Crashing on foam, with all their might.
Each wipeout a laugh, they roll with the tide,
Making waves in the sun, oh what a delight!

Seashells gossip, 'Have you heard the news?'
Underwater parties with dancing blues.
Suit up with fins, let's dive in deep,
In this salty playground, there's no time to snooze!

So grab your floaties, let's start our quest,
Splashing and laughing, it's simply the best.
As the tide sways and sings its tune,
We find joy in every watery jest.

Sailboats on a Golden Horizon

Sailboats wiggle, like they're in a race,
Tugging and swaying, oh what a pace!
With kites up high, they howl and cry,
As the wind cracks jokes, in this sunny place.

Onlookers giggle at the patterned fleet,
With bright stripes and spots, oh what a treat!
While sails flap with joy, like they're alive,
In this canvas of laughter, it's hard to beat.

The captain shouts, 'Hold steady, my crew!'
As they fish for fun, turning old into new.
But the wind plays tricks and creates a mix,
In a world where even anchors turn blue.

So cast away worries, let's sail away,
Riding the ripples of joy today.
With sunsets painting smiles, hearts fill up fast,
In this silly regatta, laughter's our way.

Sunlit Shores and Whispering Palms

Upon the sands I find my toes,
A crab scuttles past, oh how it goes!
Seagulls squawk, a cheeky flight,
Stealing fries from kids with delight.

Beach balls bounce with joyous cheer,
A flip-flop flies, oh dear, oh dear!
Sandy sandwiches, far from neat,
The laughter echoes, oh what a treat!

With sunscreen smeared on every face,
We dance in waves, a slippery race!
A sunburnt nose, a sight to see,
We laugh and pose, just you and me.

At dusk we gather, stories to share,
Of jellyfish stings and oceanal dare.
The night creeps in, we lose our grip,
The ocean's allure, a funny trip!

Where the Ocean Kisses the Land

Waves come crashing, splashing high,
A runaway hat soars to the sky.
Surfboards wobble, laughter swells,
As someone tumbles, oh, how it yells!

Sandcastles rise, a royal throne,
Until a wave calls it homegrown.
Shells are treasures, or so we think,
One's a shoehorn, who needs a link?

Beach games start with a mighty cheer,
But wait, my drink just disappeared!
A seagull snatched it, what a tease,
Now, all I've got is the salty breeze.

As the sun dips low in the bay,
We hold our drinks, come what may.
With towel tunics in goofy style,
We celebrate our beachside guile!

Mango Dreams and Crystal Waters

Mango smoothies drip down my chin,
Yummy delights, where to begin?
Splashing in pools, smiles on our face,
A floaty ring, I'm racing in place!

Crystal waters call with a gleam,
But diving in turns into a scream.
A splash on my back, what was that?
Oh look, a kid with a soggy hat!

Sunburnt laughter fills the air,
Oops! There's seaweed tangled in hair.
Fishy friends in the shallows dart,
As I attempt to channel my art.

Under the sun with joy so bright,
Each moment crafted pure delight.
We giggle as the day drifts away,
With mango dreams, we play and play!

Serenity Beneath the Coconut Canopy

Beneath the trees where coconuts sway,
I sip my drink and dream away.
A mischievous monkey swings on by,
Stealing my snack—oh my, oh my!

Hammocks sway in a sleepy dance,
While crabs break out in a funny prance.
Lemonade spills with a laugh and thud,
Oops! There goes a coconut bud!

With coconuts plopping like crazy rain,
We dodge and weave, amidst the playful pain.
Songs of the parrots fill the breeze,
Awkward bird calls bring us to our knees.

As stars come out beyond the fronds,
We share our tales, and then respond.
In this paradise, we find great cheer,
Life's a party when friends are near!

Secrets Beneath the Mango Trees

Beneath the trees, where shadows play,
A squirrel juggles nuts all day.
He drops one, makes a silly face,
Then scurries off with such a pace.

The mangoes whisper tales of delight,
As parrots dance in joyful flight.
They squawk and squabble, quite refined,
While sticky fingers seem maligned.

A hidden treasure, oh so sweet,
But bites the ants when they compete.
With laughter echoing through the leaves,
Nature's mischief weaves and weaves.

The breeze it carries giggles high,
As fruit falls down from trees nearby.
A festival of chuckles, see,
In every corner, wild and free.

Laughter on the Sandy Canvas

On sandy shores where wild waves crash,
A crab in boots makes quite a splash.
He dances 'round with speedy zeal,
While starfish giggle, oh what a deal!

A toddler builds a castle grand,
But seagulls plot a sneaky plan.
They swoop and snatch a snack or two,
While parents laugh, not quite sure what to do.

The sun is bright, the sky a fluke,
A jellyfish says, 'Let's raise a hoop!'
With every flop and funny dive,
The beach erupts, oh how they thrive!

So gear up for a silly spree,
And join the fun with glee and glee.
For laughter on the shores so wide,
Is where good moods will always bide.

Driftwood Stories of the Sea

Upon the shore, driftwood lies still,
But wait! It starts a tale to fill.
A wise old log with knots galore,
Says, 'I've seen more than a fisherman's score!'

A fish in shorts swims by with flair,
Sings tales of treasure, oh how rare!
But he gets tangled in seaweed threads,
As laughter bubbles from all the heads.

The octopus, with eight arms flailing,
Claims it can dance while boaters are bailing.
With a wink and twirl, it swings around,
And even mermaids can't help but be bound.

The sea is alive with zany charms,
Where every wave comes with new alarms.
So gather 'round this ocean's room,
And let the stories make you zoom!

Vibrant Flora and Gentle Breeze

In a garden bursting with colors bright,
A bee in sunglasses takes a flight.
It buzzes tunes, a little dance,
While flowers sway, lost in a trance.

A chubby caterpillar in a hat,
Proclaims it's cool, can you imagine that?
While ladybugs roll on flower beds,
And chuckle softly as they spread.

The breeze it tickles every petal neat,
As flowers blush in the summer heat.
With every gust, a giggle flows,
And nature joins the silly shows.

So frolic through this playful scene,
Where laughter reigns, and joy's routine.
In vibrant colors, mischief will tease,
Beneath the leaves and gentle breeze.

Serenity in Hibiscus

In the garden, blooms so bright,
A flower smirks, it's quite a sight.
Bees in bow ties buzz around,
Sipping nectar, making sound.

The sun may rise, it's quite a tease,
But shade is found beneath the trees.
A lizard grins upon a rock,
As kids chase bubbles in a flock.

The breeze brings laughter, light, and cheer,
As mango pirates dance near here.
Hibiscus hats and sunglasses wide,
We giggle in this joy-filled ride.

Laughter echoes through the coast,
In this paradise, we love the most.
With every sip of coconut dreams,
Life's just as silly as it seems.

Mango Melodies

Mangoes tumbling, rolling down,
A fruity circus in this town.
Sunset drips like honey gold,
The trees hide stories yet untold.

A parrot squawks a silly tune,
Underneath the cheeky moon.
Swaying hips from trees above,
Dance along to mango love.

With every slice, a joy parade,
Sticky fingers, no charade.
Laughter echoes, oh so sweet,
With every vibrant, juicy treat.

Umbrellas twirl, drinks are poured,
This fruity frenzy we adore.
In the grove, we find our song,
Every moment, where we belong.

Dance of the Fireflies

In the twilight, lights take flight,
Tiny dancers in the night.
Flickering tales they weave with grace,
In the dark, they find their place.

Jumping frogs join in the show,
Croaks and chirps in soft echo.
Laughter spills like lemonade,
In this rhythm, we have made.

With lanterns lit, we chase the fun,
While finding stars, one by one.
Fireflies wink, a spark, a tease,
We twirl and leap, such sweet unease.

Underneath the laughing sky,
Bubbles float and wishes fly.
In every glow, we feel alive,
With happy hearts, we dance and jive.

Paradise Found in Every Breeze

The breeze brings whispers, sweet and sly,
Like secrets slipped from clouds that fly.
Palm trees sway, a goofy dance,
While sand crabs play their little prance.

A piña colada spills with cheer,
As seashells gossip, loud and clear.
Children giggle, chased by waves,
Building castles, the ocean saves.

Squirrels steal a sip on the sly,
Yet no one seems to bat an eye.
The sun-baked laughter fills the air,
In this slice of bliss, we have flair.

Every gust, a tickling sigh,
While umbrellas bow and waves reply.
So here we toast and make our stand,
In nature's humor, hand in hand.

Lullabies of the Surf and Sand

Waves crash down with a goofy grin,
Sandcastles wobble, it's a win-win.
Seagulls squawk like they own the shore,
While sunscreen's applied, oh what a chore!

Children giggle, run, and slide,
Daddies tumble, letting pride abide.
Flip-flops flung with a joyful squeal,
Beachball battles, oh, the zeal!

Sunsets blush with marshmallow hues,
Kites zigzag like they've hit the snooze.
Pineapple juice spills, a sticky trap,
And everyone's caught in a sunburn nap!

Crabs scuttle like they're winning a race,
Footprints dance, all over the place.
With laughter echoing, the day's delight,
Lullabies play as stars peek at night.

Hidden Coves and Gentle Tides

We found a cove where mermaids sing,
Sardines swim, and lobsters bling!
But watch out for the seaweed prank,
Once you're tangled, you can't just yank!

Breezy hats take a flying leap,
While sunburned tour guides navigate deep.
Pineapples bob, in floats they swirl,
And jellyfish dance with a friendly twirl!

Tidal waves come in a silly dance,
Flip-flops lost give the ocean a chance.
Tandem paddle then take a spill,
With giggles and chuckles, it's quite the thrill!

Seashells gossip like old friends do,
While turtle races soon ensue.
Hidden treasures like ice cream cones,
Turned into sticky, sweet beachy tones!

Heartbeats in the Heart of Nature

Chirping frogs sing a too-loud song,
While butterflies flit with a dance so wrong.
A raccoon waves, with an acorn prize,
While bears practice their awkward hi-fives!

Squirrels debate on which nut to choose,
As laughter bubbles like a fizzy booze.
Caterpillars wobble, ballet on the go,
And flowers giggle with each gentle blow!

Woodpeckers knock like they're at the door,
While trees whisper secrets, just a bit more.
Kites in the sky look down with surprise,
"Nature's a stand-up!" they jest with their flies.

In the thicket, echoes of joy bounce low,
Bees buzz merrily, putting on a show.
With every heart and every root,
Nature's laughter becomes the sweetest fruit!

Secrets Shared Under Starlit Skies

Underneath stars that twinkle and tease,
Whispers drift softly on a warm summer breeze.
Marshmallows roasting create silly tunes,
As owls hoot softly, blowing away moons.

Flashlights flicker like fireflies' dance,
While shadows play games that make all hearts prance.
Campfire stories turn wild and weird,
With laughter like candy, it's all we've cheered!

Night creatures gossip, their tales quite tall,
About the traveler who tripped and did fall.
Canoes drift by under views that shine,
Where friendship blooms; a sweet, silly vine!

Guided by stars in a giggly spree,
We tiptoe through dreams, just you and me.
Secrets abound in this night of delight,
Where laughter paints colors and skies feel just right.

Rhythms of the Island Breeze

Palm trees sway, a dance so bright,
Monkeys swing, what a funny sight!
Coconuts drop, a thudding sound,
And tourists giggle just all around.

Flip-flops slap on the sunlit sand,
A crab scuttles, oh isn't he grand?
Hula lessons gone a bit wrong,
Laughter echoes, we all sing along.

Ice cream melts as kids start to fight,
"Mine's the best!" sparks a joyful plight.
Seagulls swoop with mischievous glee,
Stealing fries, oh what a spree!

As sunsets blend in hues so wild,
Sip some punch, be nature's child.
Dance and play, forget all woes,
Embrace the laughter, let it flow.

Paradise Found in Coral Gardens

Underwater giggles, fish that glow,
Coral castles where sea turtles flow.
A clam snaps shut, what a surprise,
Maybe it's hiding, who knows? Who's wise?

Snorkel masks on, ready to dive,
Explorers cheer, "We're truly alive!"
Bubbles rise in a merry dance,
Each wave brings laughter, oh what a chance!

Seaweed tickles our toes with glee,
"Look out!" someone yells, "There's a bee!"
But it's just a fish with a very wide grin,
Next stop, the beach, let the fun begin!

Shells we collect, odd shapes abound,
Each one a treasure, surprises found.
With stories to tell, back to shore we race,
Joyful antics in this fun-filled place.

The Sweet Aroma of Summer Rain

Thunder rumbles, but it's not so grim,
A splash fight starts, on a whim!
Raindrops tangle in our hair,
Laughing loudly, we've not a care.

Puddles form, oh what a delight,
Jumping around, silly as night!
Rubber ducks sail in the streams,
Each says, "I'm king!" and rules the dreams.

The air is sweet, like candy confetti,
Dancing in raindrops, isn't it petty?
Friends take selfies, catching the fun,
Wishing this joy would never be done.

The sun peeks out, a rainbow appears,
Fizzing drinks, we're raising our cheers!
As laughter drips with the fading rain,
Nothing beats this funny refrain.

Sunsets Paint the Evening Sky

Golden rays spill like melted ice,
Fireflies twinkle, an enchanting spice.
Kids chase shadows, laughing so loud,
As evening paints us like a bright cloud.

Picnic baskets, oh what a sight,
A sandwich fight, who'll win tonight?
With jelly on our noses, we cheer,
These silly moments we hold dear.

As the sun dips low, a cheeky tease,
The sky erupts in colors that please.
"More pink!" one shouts, "Let's mix it right!"
Artists in jest, we paint the night.

So let's toast marshmallows, watch the stars,
Count the funny shapes, near and far.
In every giggle, every little sigh,
We find our magic in the evening sky.

Embracing the Warmth of Sunbeams

Sunbeams hugging my sunscreened face,
I slipped on the beach, what a graceful case!
Seagulls mock my clumsy ballet,
As the breeze steals my sandwich away.

With every sip of my coconut cheer,
I found a squirrel, now I'm the deer!
A flip-flop flings, oh where did it land?
I blame those waves for a lack of a hand!

Bikini clad friends strike poses so bold,
While I try to hide a sunburn untold.
We laugh at the footprints we make in the sand,
Competing to see who can dance like a band!

The sun sets, cocktails toast in the light,
While tales of our follies bring evening delight.
With each little spill and laughter we share,
Life's simply a joy when you're free as the air!

Lush Meadows of Emerald Green

In emerald fields, we bounce like a ball,
Chasing after butterflies, stumbling, we fall.
Giggles erupt as I trip on a vine,
Nature's own prank—oh, isn't it fine?

My friends roll past in a merry pig pile,
While I point and laugh, not caring my style.
Ants join the party, they're having a blast,
But I scream in delight—a picnic amassed!

The trees wave their arms like a dance-off, you see,
While I try to boogie, just watch me be free.
Each step is a whirl, I'm the meadow-dancing queen,
With daisies as crowns, oh what a scene!

As the sun kisses grass with a tender goodnight,
We roll on the ground, our hearts feeling light.
In this zany adventure, what fun we create,
Emerald dreams, oh isn't life great?

A Dance of Waves and Swaying Silhouettes

Waves dance around, a raucous parade,
I'm caught in the tide, my plans all delayed.
With a flip and a splash, oh what a surprise,
I emerge with seaweed that covers my eyes!

Swaying like sea grass, I'm lost in the fun,
The sun is my witness, oh what have I done?
My friends cheer me on, while they point and they laugh,
That splashing mad folly—what a weird path!

Ocean's rhythm pulls us deeper in play,
While crabs pinch our toes, oh what a cliché!
We stumble, we fall, like ships lost in fate,
Yet with giggles and shouts, we embrace this strange state.

As twilight wraps us in a cozy embrace,
Our silhouettes flicker in a wild chase.
One last splash and a laugh, our giggles take flight,
With waves as our music, we dance through the night!

Golden Sands and Endless Horizons

Golden sands stretch like a flaky pastry,
I'd find a perfect spot, but it's never hasty.
As I dig in the sand, a castle appears,
But seagulls befriend me, my work disappears!

Tanned backs turning like wayward ships,
My attempts to relax lead to silly slips.
With beach balls flying and laughter that grows,
I find a new talent—like sand cupatos!

A sunburn so fierce, it could rival the sun,
Each shade of red screams, "This is lots of fun!"
But the ocean's embrace calls my worries away,
With silly surf duels brightening the day.

As the sun bows low over horizons aglow,
With hearts ever light, we twirl in a show.
In this land of giggles, where joys come alive,
Golden sands giggle back, oh how we thrive!

Islands of Clouded Fantasies

On islands made of cotton candy,
The palm trees dance; it's quite dandy.
With piña coladas for every meal,
The fruit bats plotting their next big steal.

Seagulls squawk in a comical tune,
While sunbathers sunbathe on a reggae balloon.
The sand is warm, but oh so sticky,
And my flip-flops find humor in being picky.

In coconut shells, we drink our tea,
Sipping slowly, like it's meant to be.
The crabs hold court in a sandy bar,
Telling jokes that travel quite far.

As sunsets paint the skies so bright,
We giggle under the fading light.
In these clouded dreams afloat we stay,
Where laughter's the main dish today.

Harmonies of Shore and Sky

The waves hum tunes of lazy delight,
While surfers dance, toppling in flight.
Mermen juggling seashells with glee,
Shouting, "Look at me!" like it's easy peasy.

A parrot sings in a feathered coat,
While fish swim by in a comical boat.
Tropical snacks, oh what a sight!
Pineapples glued to the surfboards tight.

Shells march in a synchronized line,
With snails on drums, they keep the time.
Seashells giggle as they tumble and roll,
In this coastal concert, we've found our soul.

Breezes tease us with gentle whispers,
Tickling our toes like playful whiskers.
In harmonies of blue and gold,
We dance and sing, becoming bold.

A Blanket of Stars

Under a quilt of twinkling light,
We tell tales of the starfish fight.
Pineapples wear confused grins,
While seahorses debate their fins.

Fireflies dance in the salty air,
Each flicker brings a surprising flair.
The moon's a lighthouse, guiding the way,
For lost flip-flops that went out to play.

We lie on the sand, seeking the best,
Dreaming of splashes, and seafood fest.
"Eh, is that a comet?" we laugh and cheer,
Nope, just a coconut rolling near.

In this whimsical, starlit embrace,
Laughter bubbles up, a warm, gentle grace.
Count the stars, one, two, three, four,
While giggles hide behind every shore.

Leafy Lullabies

In the jungle, problems fade away,
As monkeys play hopscotch all day.
Bananas are hats, quite the trend,
And every sloth is your new best friend.

Leaves rustle softly, composing a score,
A leafy lullaby you simply adore.
Frogs in togas jump and jive,
Sharing sticky notes on how to thrive.

Pineapple parties, oh what a scene!
Dancing like nobody's quite ever seen.
Fishes throw confetti from the sea,
And sing along, "This is the life, whee!"

In this leafy haven, blooms abound,
With laughter ringing, a glorious sound.
So, let's sway with the vines, have a blast,
For here, my friend, the good times last.

Deserted Coves and Hidden Treasures

On a beach so bright, I lost my hat,
It flew away, like a sneaky cat.
I chased it down, through sand and glee,
Turns out it landed on a giant tree.

Shells and rocks, treasures galore,
I found a shoe, but there was more!
A rum bottle with a note inside,
"Welcome to paradise, enjoy the ride!"

Sunburned noses, laughter in waves,
Surfboards crash like overzealous knaves.
We laughed so hard, the crabs joined in,
Dancing for shells, oh what a win!

Under palm trees, we set our camp,
Spotted a raccoon with a sunburnt stamp.
He mugged for pictures, a real charmer,
With a grin so goofy, it raised alarmers.

Starry Nights Under Coconut Skies

Beneath the stars, we laid so cozy,
Counting jokes, feeling quite rosy.
A coconut fell with a clumsy thud,
Rolled down the hill like a silly dud.

"Let's make wishes!" my friend did shout,
As seagulls danced and ran about.
We tossed our hopes to the sky so wide,
A crab scurried by, wearing a tide.

The moon was bright, our laughter too,
My drink spilled over, oh what a brew!
Chased by a pelican, making a scene,
With beaks all clumsy, like a sitcom queen.

The stars winked back, what a delight,
We cheered for gulls taking to flight.
One tried to steal my half-eaten fry,
I let it happen, it flew too high!

Radiant Sunsets and Sea Foam

The sun set low, a glorious sight,
We raced for the shore, oh what pure delight.
I tripped on a flip-flop, fell face-first,
Into the sand, my own little burst!

"Look out for jelly!" someone did yell,
But we were too late, under their spell.
They glowed like lanterns, quite surreal,
But we just giggled and danced a reel.

A pineapple drink spilled with a splash,
Goes to show, good times never clash.
Caught a wave not meant for my size,
Washed ashore, wearing seaweed lies!

Under the hues of fading light,
We read the clouds, not a single fright.
The sun took a bow, we waved goodbye,
Wishing for more, under the sky.

The Language of Feathered Friends

Parrots squawk, oh what a racket,
Chattering on, in a funny bracket.
One said, "Hey, did you eat that fry?"
I just nodded, full and spry.

Toucans juggled fruit on their beaks,
While we laughed at their silly techniques.
Who knew birds could throw a show?
Acting as if they're in the know!

A finch stole popcorn, flew like a pro,
Dodging the waves with a fancier flow.
They squawked and cawed, making their play,
A feathered circus to brighten the day.

As twilight crept, their dance did slow,
Birds settled down, putting on a glow.
They told us secrets, cocked their heads,
And drifted off to their cozy beds.

Forgotten Trails in Paradise

Lost my way with sunburned toes,
Chasing shadows where the coconut grows.
With a map from a flamingo's beak,
I find the path is rather bleak.

The crabs all laugh, they scuttle away,
As I trip on a very lazy stray.
In paradise, how can I complain?
Except for that sunburn, what a pain!

A parrot squawks with sheer delight,
As I dance with a coconut at night.
Forget the trails; take a seat,
Nature's punchline is quite the treat.

Cheers to laughter beneath the beams,
Where nothing's ever as it seems.
In forgotten trails, I take my spell,
With a smile and a sunburn—oh so swell!

Sunkissed Steps on Soft Sand

Woke up late, my watch is fried,
Dancing on the beach like a sunburned guide.
My flip-flops squeak, a catchy tune,
As I stumble under a bright balloon.

Seagulls peck at my cheesy snack,
I try to run, but my flip-flops lack.
With every step, I leave a trail,
Of sunscreen, giggles, and a funny tale.

The beach ball flies, a wild ride,
I catch it midair, but then I slide.
Into a patch of wet seaweed,
That's one for the books, surely agreed!

With sunkissed steps, I own the sand,
Every tumble is wonderfully planned.
So here I am, a mess of laughter,
My beachy life is happily after!

Beneath the Radiant Canopy

Underneath the trees, I seize the day,
Wrestling vines that come out to play.
A monkey grins, gives me a cheeky wink,
As I ponder my next move, or maybe a drink.

The wind whispers jokes in the palm trees,
While I dodge falling coconuts with ease.
"Is that a bird or just my hat?"
Nature's a joker, can you believe that?

Swinging from vines, like Tarzan at best,
But all I do is tumble and jest.
Lands in a patch of very soft grass,
Nature laughs so hard it's a class!

Beneath the canopy, a chaotic fun,
With trees as my allies, I'm never done.
In this wild world, I'm the punchline free,
A jester at heart, with glee and spree!

Paradise in a Single Breath

With one deep breath, I taste the scene,
A tropical smoothie that feels like a dream.
Strawberries giggle; pineapples tease,
In this fruity oasis, I aim to please.

Breath of fresh air, oh what a blast,
But wait, is that a bee zooming past?
I swat and I duck in acrobatic flair,
Turns out I'm just the local fair!

Sipping my drink, I make a toast,
To the flavors here that I love the most.
With every gulp, a joke on my tongue,
In paradise found, my laughter's up strong.

So here's the deal in this sunny spot,
Life's a big buffet, better eat a lot.
In a single breath, I find pure cheer,
With a grin on my face, bring on the beer!

The Rhythm of Ocean Waves

The ocean hums a silly tune,
As crabs do their quirky dance,
Waves wiggle like a goofy loon,
In this beachy, blissful trance.

Seagulls try to steal my fries,
While I laugh and swat at flies,
Gliding breezes share my sighs,
Underneath the sunny skies.

Sandcastles lean, then they fall,
Like my friend who gives a call,
We build them big, then let them sprawl,
What a wild, sandy brawl!

With every splash and joyful cheer,
We giggle like kids, never fear,
Ebbing waves hold memories dear,
As the ocean's pulse draws near.

Island Melodies: A Serenade

On the beach, a ukulele strums,
While tourists dance and samba hums,
Little fish do funny jumps,
Moving to the island drums.

Palm trees sway with laughter loud,
As I try to blend with the crowd,
A sunburned nose is my proud shroud,
In this bright, tropical cloud.

Hammocks swing like gentle pies,
Where my dreams go for a rise,
Coconuts roll and flirt with skies,
As I wear my goofy guise.

Seashells talk in whispers sweet,
Telling tales of friendly feet,
With crustaceans that can't be beat,
Island fun: our favorite treat.

Beneath the Coconut Canopy

Underneath this leafy dome,
A squirrel steals someone's ice-cream cone,
Birds chirp jokes like they're in a tome,
In this sweet, sunny home.

Coconuts swing, they drop and land,
Maybe they hid in the sand,
We laugh, we point, it's really grand,
Life's too fun to be quite bland.

Tanned folks nap in a sunny glut,
While one wakes up to a small coconut,
Beneath the trees, we smile and strut,
In our paradise, we're never cut.

One hammock holds a fluffy dog,
Whistling tunes, he sure can hog,
As palm leaves wave, like a green fog,
Creating a playful, breezy bog.

Graffiti of Sunset Sky

When the sky puts on a show,
Splashes of color in a row,
We watch as day takes a bow,
Painting joy for all to know.

Clouds giggle in peach and blue,
Matching the waves, a splendid view,
As evening brings a cheeky crew,
Who dare to dance, oh so askew!

Here comes the moon, don't be shy,
It winks at fish swimming by,
Stars join in, they start to fly,
In this whimsical, starlit sky.

So let's toast to the setting sun,
With fruity drinks, oh what fun,
Laughter lingers, love's begun,
A vibrant close to day's run.

A Tapestry of Color and Calm

Bright parrots squawk with glee,
While fish dance in the sea.
Coconuts fall with a thud,
As I dive straight in the mud.

The sun wears shades so cool,
As I splash in the pool.
A hammock swings, oh what a sight,
It's nap time—what a delight!

My fruit hat starts to sway,
As I laugh the sun away.
Palm trees whisper silly songs,
In this place where joy belongs.

With laughter and sunshine's glow,
Let the good times overflow!
In this patch of paradise,
We'll dance, we'll joke, oh what a slice!

Laughter Echoes Through Bamboo Groves

Bamboo bends with chuckles loud,
As giggles gather a curious crowd.
Monkey swings as if on zoom,
Creating mischief in every room.

A parrot mimics my silly dance,
While I leap in a clumsy prance.
The breeze carries my hearty guffaw,
As I tumble, oh what a flaw!

Against the trees, I start to trip,
With laughter, I take a dip.
Nature's friends join in the fun,
While the setting sun begins to run.

At dusk, the stars play peek-a-boo,
While I bring my friends a brew.
Laughter echoes, never a bore,
In these bamboo groves, we'll roar!

Saltwater Echoes of Joyful Days

Waves crash in a playful hug,
While I skip like a happy bug.
The salty air tickles my nose,
As I chase crabs, oh how it goes!

Seagulls squawk as if to jest,
As I dive in like it's a quest.
Sandcastles wobble, oh dear me,
But laughter saved them, can't you see?

Beach balls bounce in silly arcs,
While kids splash, leaving bright marks.
The sun burns bright, but we don't care,
Under umbrellas, we'll share a chair.

As the sunset paints the sky,
We gather round with a hearty sigh.
Songs of joy in salty air,
In these moments, nothing can compare!

Nature's Symphony in Verdant Harmony

In the jungle, drums go boom,
While frogs croak their joyful tune.
Vines swing 'round as I stomp,
With silly moves, oh what a romp!

Bees buzz like they're in a race,
Pollen flying all over the place.
Leaves rustle with laughter in tow,
As I weave through this vibrant glow.

A lizard winks, oh what a sight,
As butterflies take flight at night.
Crickets chirp in rhythmic beats,
As I dance with my two left feet.

In this lush green, life unfolds,
With stories of joy, yet untold.
Nature's symphony plays on and on,
With laughter resonating until dawn!

Whispers of the Palm Leaves

Beneath the palms, a breeze fills the air,
Coconuts tumble, oh what a scare!
Parrots gossip, they squawk with delight,
While I trip over sandals, what a sight!

A squirrel steals my sandwich with a grin,
Climbs up a tree, that cheeky little kin.
Monkeys swing down, they want a taste too,
I'll leave the fruit, take the sandwich—who knew?

Sandy crabs dance as they shuffle on by,
Wiggling their pincers, oh me, oh my!
I share a laugh with a sunburnt old chap,
As we both lay back for a midday nap.

Here in the sun, no worries be found,
Just giggles and laughter, pure joy all around.
With a drink in hand and toes in the sand,
I'll take this chaos, oh isn't it grand?

Sunlit Shores at Dusk

The sun dips low, a painter's last stroke,
Seagulls laugh at each silly folk.
Sandcastles topple, oh what a mess,
But kids just giggle, they can't care less.

Surfboards gather as the night draws near,
One wipes out badly, while everyone cheers!
A crab takes a stroll, so proud and so bold,
With tiny pinchers, he's braver than most old.

Bonfire's lit, the marshmallows toast,
Someone's singing—oh, it's quite the boast!
But with one big bite, they fall in the sand,
Sweet sticky mess, oh it wasn't planned.

Laughter erupts, it echoes the shore,
With each little blunder, we love it more.
As dusk turns to night, we cherish the fun,
In this silly paradise, we are all one.

Lush Canopy Dreams

In the jungle's green, where giggles resound,
A toucan tells jokes that astound.
Monkeys mimicking my every move,
Got tangled in vines, they're still in the groove.

Kangaroos hopping, but there's no fun,
When one takes a leap and lands on the run.
They bounce and they laugh, it's quite the show,
As I'm dodging their feet, feeling quite low.

Lizards in shades dress to impress,
Strut past the flowers, causing some stress.
They're wearing their smiles, not caring a bit,
About the big sloth who's having a fit.

Hammocks are swinging with friends gathered 'round,
Sharing wild tales of each faceplant we've found.
Under the stars, with a giggle and grin,
In this vibrant dream, let the laughter begin.

Waves Kissing the Coral

The waves roll in, a soft little fuss,
Splashing my feet with a ticklish rush.
Fish peek out, like they're saying hello,
While I trip in the surf, and put on a show.

Starfish are lounging, trying to tan,
A crab with odd moves, has a wild plan.
Jumping from rocks with a silly little bounce,
Though everyone knows, he won't make a pounce.

Seashells are giggling as I gather them near,
One whispers softly, 'You look quite queer!'
But I just chuckle, for I've lost the plot,
In this vibrant playground, who cares a lot?

With laughter like waves that dance on the shore,
We bask in the silliness and seek out more.
As the sun sets low, we relish the fun,
In our whimsical world, we're all just one.

Rainbow after the Rain

Puddles gleam like shiny gems,
Wipe your feet and grab some friends.
Look up high, it's quite the show,
A colorful arc starts to glow.

Jumping in to catch a rainbow,
But instead you land in mud, oh no!
Laughter echoes in the wet,
A squishy slip, but no regret.

Clouds have parted, sun's a tease,
Chasing rainbows, feeling free.
Kites get tangled in a tussle,
The sky calls, let's all be a hustle!

The world spins in colors bright,
Dance in puddles, what a sight!
Forget your troubles, just have fun,
Giggle with friends under the sun.

Cherished Moments on the Beach

Sandy toes and sunburned noses,
Ice cream drips where the sea breeze dozes.
Umbrellas shade my silly hat,
Caught in laughter, oh look at that!

Seagulls swoop with hungry cries,
As I try to eat, with a side of fries.
Sandcastles crumbling, towers down,
On this sandy stage, I wear a crown.

Splashing water, a sudden wave,
Wiped out again, oh what a knave!
Life's a beach, or so they say,
Just roll with the waves, come what may.

Sunset glimmers on water's skin,
Wrap me up in laughter's spin.
Barefoot shenanigans, all in play,
Cherished moments, day after day.

By the Shore

Footprints are our silly art,
Leading to where the fun will start.
Shells like treasures wait for me,
Let's chase the tide and feel so free.

Waves crash down like a giggle fit,
Splashing each other, who can resist?
With a flip-flop flying high,
We make memories as gulls cry.

Sand in my sandwich, oh what joy!
Building towers like a happy boy.
Friends around, sun's golden hue,
Laughing together, no worries brew.

As the sun dips below the line,
We shout and cheer, life is divine.
Another day fades, filled with cheer,
By the shore, there's nothing to fear.

Time Pauses

Watches tick but we don't care,
Coconuts fall from trees up there.
Sipping joy from a fruity cup,
Let's forget the time and just erupt.

Clocks can't measure all this fun,
Grab a friend, let's start to run!
Sand flies up, laughter's our guide,
Time takes off like the rising tide.

Sunscreen's smeared, what a sight!
Looking like a ghost in sunlight.
Belly laughs echo through the air,
Dancing to rhythms that we don't care.

Moments freeze, like pictures framed,
Wacky poses, all unashamed.
In this place where time stands still,
We laugh at life, that's our thrill.

A Symphony of Nature's Palette

Crayons melt in the sunset glow,
Painting skies with a brilliant show.
Palm trees sway like they're in tune,
Under the flirtatious afternoon.

Breezes carry giggles afar,
Nature's orchestra, oh how bizarre!
A chorus of waves helping us dance,
In this moment, we take a chance.

Fish jump high with silly splashes,
We try to catch them, but it clashes.
With swings and laughter all around,
Joyful notes in every sound.

Colors swirl in breezy waves,
Nature's laughter, it never waives.
Join the symphony, feel the cheer,
In our hearts, summer is here.

The Allure of Salt-Kissed Haze

Waves giggle as they touch the shore,
Sunburns whisper, 'We'll come back for more.'
Flip-flops dance, lost in the sand,
Seagulls squawk, stealing lunch from your hand.

Coconuts fall, rolling like dice,
While sunscreen smells like a bad paradise.
Laughter echoes, travelers unite,
As crabs scuttle off, plotting to bite.

Floaties in colors that hurt the eyes,
Beach balls bounce under azure skies.
Ice cream melts down arms like a trail,
And beach hats soar high like a sail.

Bikini lines tell tales of sun,
Fried egg on a towel, a day well done.
Sunset splashes orange in a wacky way,
Hurry! Grab your cocktail—it's almost Monday!

Moments Caught in Sea Breezes

A flip-flop flops, and a smoothie spills,
Seagulls caw louder than silly shrills.
Umbrellas tilt like they've lost a bet,
While kids chase tides in a water jet.

The ocean is a dancer, swirling around,
While sunburned tourists sprawl on the ground.
Looks like a lobster? Not quite right,
But hey, you'll be tan by tomorrow night!

Wind in hair does nothing for style,
But look at that kid, surfing with a smile!
Sunscreen fights off the rays in a hoot,
While jellyfish do their snooze in the loot.

Kites are flying, one kisses a tree,
Sandcastles crumble, how funny to see!
Ice cream on noses, a sticky parade,
Oh, memories made in sunshine's charade!

Harmony Under the Canopy

Parrots squawk, making a fuss,
While I try not to trip on the bus!
Swings hung low, laughter's a must,
Watch out! The monkey's up to his rust!

Lush leaves rustle in a cheeky dance,
While squirrels engage in a nutty romance.
Picnics are set, but ants all parade,
Joining the feast, uninvited brigade!

Breezes blow softly through tangled vines,
Tickling my arms with mischievous signs.
Sunlight pierces in playful beams,
As we follow our wildest schemes.

Nature's concert plays in a silly key,
With frogs croaking off-key with glee.
Together we laugh, what a cluster of fun,
Under the canopy, we've just begun!

Meadows of Color and Light

Flowers bloom with a cheeky wink,
Bees buzzing loudly, don't stop to think.
Butterflies flutter like confetti in flight,
While daisies gossip well into the night.

Sunshine spills like lemonade sweet,
Clouds hold a race on invisible feet.
Grass tickles toes, it's pure delight,
Until you step on an ant, oh what a fright!

Picnics are messy, and look at that pie—
Just a face plant, no need to cry.
Laughter erupts when the ants take a bite,
Suddenly sharing seems just right!

Rainbows arc after a playful shower,
While flowers dance under skies that empower.
A meadow of color, how splendid and bright,
Crafting our joy, from day into night!

Radiance of the Midsummer Sun

The sun's so bright, it's like a cheer,
My ice cream's melting, oh dear,
Sand in my shorts, what a delight,
I'll dance around like a bird in flight.

With sunglasses on, I strut my stuff,
Beach balls bouncing, that's good enough,
Seagulls squawk, steal my lunch,
I wave goodbye; they're in for a crunch!

The waves crash down, they've got great aim,
Tidal splashes, it's a wild game,
Flip-flops flying, I lose a shoe,
But who needs both? I'll manage, it's true!

My friend says let's do a cannonball,
But I just flop; I'm not graceful at all,
Splashing everyone, giggles arise,
Under the sun, laughter never lies.

The Gentle Touch of Ocean Spray

Ocean whispers secrets in my ear,
A gentle splash brings a giggle near,
I dive in headfirst, what a disaster,
But the waves keep coming, a teasing master.

My hair is a mess, like seaweed found,
The tide rolls in with a comical sound,
Laughing at crabs, they scuttle away,
Who knew they could dance? What a display!

The lifeguard watches like a noble knight,
As I attempt to float, drift left, then right,
With a splash and a laugh, I sink like a stone,
Yet rise with a grin, I'm never alone!

Salt on my lips, sand in my swim,
Life feels so silly, I can't help but grin,
The ocean's embrace is such a delight,
In this watery world, everything feels right.

Reflections by the Shore

Mirrored in waves, I see my face,
Sunburned nose, oh what a grace,
As I strike poses, I feel so fine,
A beachside model, sipping on brine.

Footprints left, a silly parade,
Chasing the tide as it swiftly fades,
Seashells whisper under my toes,
Nature's confetti, in my beachy woes.

The sandcastles wobble, oh what a sight,
A king without castles, but hey, that's alright,
Giggling seagulls steal my snack,
I guess they're the rulers; I face the lack!

With every splash, my laughter soars,
Forgetting the world, I just want more,
Under the sun, forever we play,
Living these moments, come what may.

A Canvas of Brilliant Colors

Splashes of paint inspire my muse,
Umbrellas twirling, choose any hues,
The sky in orange, pink, and blue,
Like a toddler's drawing, that's how I view.

Flip-flops in sync as we dance around,
With each vibrant shade, joy knows no bound,
Banana boats float, who wobbles more?
If I tip over, it's laughter galore!

Cocktails in hand, with cherries on top,
Sipping too slowly; they bubble and pop,
A pineapple hat? Oh, what a treat!
Fashion so quirky, I dance to the beat.

Boys on the sand, building their dreams,
While girls in bright dresses share ice cream schemes,
Under this canvas, we blend and we play,
Creating bright memories, come join the fray!

A Canvas of Waves and Sunlight

The sun wears shades, quite a sight,
A beach ball bounces, oh what a flight!
Flip-flops dance with a sandy tune,
While jellyfish waltz beneath the moon.

Seagulls squawk like they're in a band,
Surfboards lined up, it's totally planned.
With sunscreen dashed on like war paint,
Let's catch some rays, or fish, or faint!

Drinks with umbrellas, looking so neat,
To sip and spill—oh, what a treat!
Sandcastle dreams that may just collapse,
We laugh as they fall; oh boy, what mishaps!

Here comes the tide with a cheeky wave,
To tickle our toes—the ocean's our rave!
Life's a beach party, so join the dance,
With all of nature given the chance!

The Allure of the Hidden Lagoon

In a jungle thick, with colors so bright,
A secret lagoon comes to greet the light.
With fish that poke out, like they want to chat,
And frogs doing flips in a big hat.

Vines swing 'round like they're in a race,
While monkeys swing by, showing off their grace.
Pink blooms giggle like they just got a joke,
While turtles bask and ponder then croak.

The water's like jelly, oh what a treat,
With splashes and giggles, it's hard to beat!
We dive in and swim, but alas, what a fail,
As a fish gives us wedgies—oh, the tale!

At sunset, we toast to the day's silly fun,
With a fruit that's squishy, and where's my bun?
The hidden lagoon—our laughter, our song,
In nature's embrace, where we all belong!

Breezy Days and Starry Nights

The breeze is a trickster, blowing hats away,
And my hair's a scandal—it won't obey!
A kite flies high, like it knows a secret,
While my sandwich feels lost, like it's not a meat on a becket.

Stars twinkle down like they're playing charades,
While crickets serenade—aren't they fond of parades?
The moon's pouting, it's lost its glow,
Could it be jealous of a firefly show?

We roast marshmallows; they catch fire, oh dear,
As laughter erupts, fueling our cheer.
Each snapping twig dances to the beat,
In this world of wonder, it's hard to stay neat!

As morning arrives, with the songs of the dawn,
Nature's wild theater, where giggles are drawn.
Breezy days leading to nights full of glee,
In this silly, soft rhythm, we're forever carefree!

A Sanctuary of Serenity and Sunshine

In a hammock that swings like it's had too much fun,
I nap in the shade, while the world's on the run.
Birds show off dances, with a twist and a twirl,
While ants march on by, giving it a whirl.

A picnic of snacks, that ants commandeer,
Where's my sandwich? Now, I shed a small tear.
But the bees they are buzzing a sweet little song,
While my best friends are laughing; it just feels so wrong!

Palm trees wiggle like they've got the moves,
While butterflies gossip about all their grooves.
The sun drops low, and I'd love a snack,
But the chipmunks are in, they won't cut me slack!

Serenity reigns, though it may seem absurd,
As chaos creates, laughter's the word.
In this sanctuary, where we all gear up,
To sip on the sunshine from a happy cup!

www.ingramcontent.com/pod-product-compliance
Lightning Source LLC
Chambersburg PA
CBHW072218070526
44585CB00015B/1393